T0110554

SULPICIAE ELIGIAE

THE LIFE, TIMES AND WORKS OF A ROMAN WOMAN

M.E. RANDALL

Sulpiciae Eligiae
The Life, Times and Works of a Roman Woman

Copyright © 2010, 2016 M.E. Randall.

All rights reserved. No part of this book may be used or reproduced by any means, graphic, electronic, or mechanical, including photocopying, recording, taping or by any information storage retrieval system without the written permission of the author except in the case of brief quotations embodied in critical articles and reviews.

iUniverse books may be ordered through booksellers or by contacting:

iUniverse
1663 Liberty Drive
Bloomington, IN 47403
www.iuniverse.com
1-800-Authors (1-800-288-4677)

Because of the dynamic nature of the Internet, any web addresses or links contained in this book may have changed since publication and may no longer be valid. The views expressed in this work are solely those of the author and do not necessarily reflect the views of the publisher, and the publisher hereby disclaims any responsibility for them.

Any people depicted in stock imagery provided by Thinkstock are models, and such images are being used for illustrative purposes only.
Certain stock imagery © Thinkstock.

ISBN: 978-1-4502-5598-1 (sc)
ISBN: 978-1-4502-5599-8 (e)

Print information available on the last page.

iUniverse rev. date: 03/30/2016

CUI DONO LEPIDUM NOVUM LIBELLUM..........
MEI DISCIPULI

CONTENTS

FORWARD

This work was inspired by my continual desire and passion to be infused with information about the history of ancient Rome. But as I quickly learned in my undergraduate studies, if I wanted to understand history, it was essential to be an interdisciplinary student. I needed to be a dedicated learner of subjects like sociology, etymology, and anthropology if I were ever going to truly understand the history of ancient Rome.

In light of this, after teaching Latin for two years, I quickly became aware of the need to elucidate, or bring to life, the different and often neglected aspects of ancient Rome-- Roman women. For my middle school and high school students, creating a fair and balanced learning experience became my main goal. The majority of my students were teenage girls, and as my mother had always taught me to be conscientious of the "marginalized" group of people, I couldn't help but wonder what must be going through the minds of these girls when they read the overabundant writings of male chauvinists.

Thus, I believe that the middle school and high school Latin classes of today must reflect the interdisciplinary nature of Classical Studies. In order to grow the Latin language in the private and public schools of America, I feel the language must be taught through a male and *female* perspective. Though the female voice in ancient Rome was meant for the most part to be silenced, Classicists must do their best to shed light on the feminine perspective in Ancient Rome. It is with this purpose that I have spent a little over a year creating this work for my Latin students.

INTRODUCTION

Not enough attention is given to Roman women in current Latin texts. Although the corpus of Latin works by Roman women is limited, undoubtedly presenting the Classicist with challenges of what to expound and elucidate, sufficient effort must be made in order to create a balanced picture of Ancient Roman life. Such an insight would give students in middle schools and high schools accurate and invaluable information about the lives of Roman women.

This small book of the writings of the Augustan Sulpicia introduces the young Latin student to the sophisticated and eloquent poetry of one of Rome's most readable poets, especially for students at the intermediate to advanced Latin stage. This book is divided into three sections: "The Life of Sulpicia," "Catullus and His Influence on Sulpicia" and "The Elegies." In the first section of the book, "The Life of Sulpicia," the reader is given a historical and biographical sketch of her life and times. The intent of this section is to show the reader that she was a well-educated and highly sophisticated Roman woman who just happened to live during the tumultuous times of the Republican Civil Wars.

The primary intention of the book is to function as a supplemental reader coinciding historically, chronologically, and grammatically with the Oxford Latin Course The Oxford Latin text retells the life of the satirist and poet Quintus Horatius Flaccus, known in English as Horace. Some historians have suggested that Sulpicia may have been in the literary circle of Horace; therefore the book acts as a valuable learning tool by introducing Latin students to a contemporary poet of Horace. However, this is not the sole intent. This book would add succinct quality to any Latin class. My teaching experience has shown me that the student's enjoy reading about the life of Horace, but lack original Latin passages that are accessible and interesting-- this book fills that need.

In the second section of the book, "Catullus and His Influence on Sulpicia," the reader is introduced to the literary genre known as Neoteric poetics, of which Sulpicia's works could be classified. The reader learns about the genius of the Greeks, specifically Callimachus, and how his poetry affected the young poets who were under the patronage of Maecenas—most notably Catullus. Arguably, the most widely known Latin poet of this style was Catullus. The reader is introduced to his writings and the many ways in which the Greek poetic style influenced his writings and in turn Sulpicia.

In the third section of the book, "The Elegies," the reader encounters five of Sulpicia's six elegies. Her works are short in nature and are often given no title, but rather a number, such as Elegy 1, and the like. For the sake of clarity and for the sake of purpose, each elegy or poem has been given a title which corresponds to the theme of each poem. A glossary and index of words for reference are provided as an aid for translating located at the end of the book. Below each line of an elegy, or poem, is a considerable amount of space, which provides a sufficient area for students to write their translations or notes.

Also in Section III after each poem are exercises and questions for students to complete as an assessment. The questions range from parsing exercises, to questions requiring students to analyze Sulpicia's feelings, thoughts, etc.

Thus, with each completed section, the student increases his or her understanding of Rome's most influential female writers. Her poetry enables students to understand the mind of a Roman woman and gives an important point of view that is often not accessible through a traditional Latin course of study.

SECTION I

THE LIFE OF SULPICIA

CHILDHOOD AND EDUCATION

Sulpicia was born to a wealthy family from Etruria just north of the city of Rome.[1] She was probably born sometime between 55 to 45 B.C.E., though the exact date is uncertain. Her father, Servius Sulpicius Rufus, a member of the Lemonian tribe with full voting privileges in Rome, was a friend and colleague of Marcus Tullius Cicero the eloquent orator and arguably the most significant politician of the Roman Republic. Servius was a well educated and well spoken man. He studied rhetoric with Cicero, but found that law suited him best. Thus, he became a successful Roman jurist and because of his family's wealth, he was influential amongst Rome's elite upper class patricians. He wrote over 180 treatises on law, though none have survived into modern times. There is one important piece of writing that has lasted over two thousand years though, and that is a copy of a letter he wrote to Cicero expressing his condolences over the death of Tulia, Cicero's daughter.[2] During his life, Servius seems to have impacted the lives of various Romans who played a key role during the tumultuous Civil Wars of the Late Roman Republic. Cicero, in one of his letters to Servius, described him as a man of wisdom and character, a true friend in times of deep sorrow, one who offers sincere condolences and is always willing to listen and converse over matters both private and public.[3]

In 63 B.C.E. Sulpicius ran for consul, but was defeated by Lucius Licinius

Murena, whom he later accused of bribery. Ironically it was his friend, Cicero who defended Murena. Sulpicius would eventually gain the consulship though twelve years later. It was during his consulship that Sulpicius had the opportunity to become better acquainted with Gaius Iulius Caesar. After much reasoning, Sulpicius decided to support Caesar against Pompey and his allies. Fortunately for Sulpicius he was rewarded by Caesar in 46 B.C.E. when he was made the proconsul of Achaea, the largest province in all of Greece.

Sulpicia's mother, Valeria, was the sister of Valerius Messalla Corvinus a friend and military ally of Augustus, however little is known about Valeria. As far as historians can tell, Sulpicia had a brother, Sulpicius, who is described in the same benevolent manner as his father by Cicero. After the death of Cicero's daughter Tulia, the younger Sulpicius visits Cicero and is described as being "kind, thoughtful, and honorable."[4] There is no other mention of her mother or brother in the annals of history.

It is perhaps through her uncle, Messalla, that Sulpicia was introduced to the wonders of Latin and Greek poetry and literature. Messalla was not only a soldier and politician; he was a lover of the arts. After the death of Sulpicius in 43 B.C.E., in the tradition of Roman *patris potestas*, Messalla became the guardian of Sulpicia. Sulpicia mentions him in *Dies Cerintho*.[5]

CHILDHOOD AND EDUCATION

As a young girl, her life was focused, from the earliest age, on learning how to manage a household with dignity and sophistication. She was given her name after her father's *gens* name, Sulpicius, converted to the feminine form. Republican patrician girls were undoubtedly trained from an early age to be good Roman wives in order to conduct the daily affairs of the household, emulating their mother, the *domina*.

Because her father and ward were patricians, she would have received a quality education. A girl's education differed in many ways to a boy's. It was expected that at an early age Roman boys and girls would attend school together. Sulpicia received her education beginning most likely at age six with an emphasis placed on studying basic grammar and arithmetic. It was the duty of the local magister or tutor to solidify the traditions and roles of patrician families. The magister was most often a Greek or well versed in the Greek language and familiar with the literature of Greece.

It was Horace who once wrote, "Captive Greece conquered her Roman conquerors." Since the Roman conquest of Greece, it became the norm for Roman elites to know both Latin and Greek. The most common method of education was divided into three stages: Elementary, Grammar and Rhetoric. For girls though, the Elementary stage was usually the highest level completed. At this stage pupils had a rudimentary and utilitarian form of education. The basic elements of reading, writing and arithmetic were taught. Students recited Latin chants and short works of poetry, but with a strong emphasis on practical daily use. Perhaps young pupils may have read small works of poetry translated from Greek or even from the *Odyssey* which was translated into the Latin by a Greek freedman named Andronicus in the third century B.C.E.

For most girls, education stopped after the first stage, however for a privileged few, education was continued through a private tutor or pedagogue.

It is highly likely that Sulpicia's education continued in this manner. In this next stage, the Grammar stage, the emphasis was on reading and writing. Literature, more specifically poetry, was the main focus. In the late Republic, pupils learned to read and write in Latin and Greek. Many works of poetry would have been available to the public. The poems of Callimachus would have been widely available. Thus women of senatorial rank were well educated; an appreciative audience for poetry, and sometimes poets themselves.[6] In Plutarch's *Life of Pompey,* he describes Cornelia, the second wife of Pompey as:

Having other attractions besides those of youth and beauty; for she was highly educated, played well upon the lute, and understood geometry, and had been accustomed to listen with profit to lectures on philosophy; all this, too, without in any degree becoming unamiable or pretentious.

Like Cornelia, Sulpicia was a daughter of senatorial rank and thus had an education worthy of that privileged class.

It also seems that Roman women enjoyed more freedom than any other ancient civilization. In the late Republic and early Empire a father could probably no longer compel his son or daughter to marry against their wills.[7] Because the legal marrying age for girls was twelve, it behooved the patrician father to find a suitable and arranged marriage in order to protect and control his daughter's dowry. If however, the father died the daughter would then gain complete control of her dowry, and if old enough, choose to be placed under the ward of a male family member. This seems to have been the case with Sulpicia being placed under the care of Messalla when her father died in 43 B.C.E.

The circumstances of Sulpicius' death are hazy at best. Cicero was convinced that Antony had had been the cause of Sulpicius' death. Sent as an ambassador for the Senate in 43 B.C.E. to Antony in Mutina, Sulpicius died while performing this duty. Though he left Italy ill, Cicero was convinced that Antony was responsible for the death of his honorable friend. In his *Philippics,* Cicero asserts that Antony neglected to care for Sulpicius, even going so far as accusing Antony of murdering him. In his speech Cicero exclaims that, "Surely he brought the man death, who was the cause of his death."[8] His rationale for this claim was elucidated by his insistence that Antony was disturbed by Sulpicius' arrival. According to Cicero, Antony outwardly showed his anger and hatred because of Sulpicius' senatorial authority. Whatever the case, Cicero successfully advocated a public funeral for his deceased friend. Perhaps this incident was the final spark in Antony's long dispute with Cicero. In that same year Antony had Cicero listed as a political enemy of the state and had his men hunt Cicero down and execute him.

WOMANHOOD AND POETICS

With the death of her father, Sulpicia was now under the ward of Messalla. In her own words, Sulpicia expresses how at times this was not a pleasant thing for her.[9] Marcus Valerius Messalla Corvinus was from one of the most well known and esteemed old patrician families. From the earliest period of Rome the Valerian family possessed and adorned the highest honors of the state.[10] Messalla lived from 64 B.C.E. to 8 C.E. In his early twenties he fought for the banner of the Republic at the battle of Philippi, became an eloquent orator befriended and praised by Cicero. Edward Gibbon describes Messalla as the cultivator of every muse, the patron of every man of genius, spending his evenings in philosophic conversation with Horace; assumed his place at the table between Delia and Tibullus, and amused his leisure by encouraging the poetical talents of young Ovid.[11]

By the time Messalla was named ward, Sulpicia would have been a young girl, and she more than likely would have been approaching the second stage of her education, whereas her new ward would have been in his early twenties just beginning his storied military career. It seems at this time also that Messalla, according to the ancient historian Jerome, married Cicero's widow Terentia. Perhaps the small age difference between herself and her ward gave Sulpicia a greater amount of freedom as the relationship dynamics were more like an older brother than a father.

Aside from being a military man, Messalla was the quintessential patrician in that he was trained to be a great public speaker or orator. At an early age Messalla was praised by many as a wonderful orator. His friend Horace places him in the first class of orators. Seneca the Elder also praised Messalla as the purest writers of his age.[12] For Sulpicia this meant that her future would now be influenced by one of Rome's most educated young leaders. From this moment on, Sulpicia would be surrounded by Rome's brightest and most brilliant young poets known as the "Neoterics." Messalla's circle of friends included Tibullus, Ovid, Horace, Catullus, and even Vergil—these men were the new generation of poets who emerged from the traumatic events of the Late Republic to produce what many call the Golden Age of Roman Literature.

Sometime between 43 and 32 B.C.E. Messalla befriended a young poet and former soldier named Tibullus. Both men, according to the historians Pliny and Plutarch were eloquent writers and lovers of poetry. Ovid calls Messalla his friend and the light and director of his literary pursuits.[13] Vergil wrote a poem called *Ciris,* in which he praised Messalla for being a great soldier, orator and poet. Though none of Messalla's works exist, his new friend Tibullus' works survived. And as was the custom of ancient society, a poet's livelihood was based upon finding a literary patron. It seems from the earliest acquaintance that Messalla and Tibullus encouraged one another in their writings, but that Messalla's duties for the state took up too much time and instead he became an avid patron of the arts choosing to support his friend Tibullus financially.

If Messalla supported his friend Tibullus, then he must have noticed his young niece's abilities as well? There is no evidence however that has come to light about how or when Sulpicia began writing or if Messalla supported her in her writing. It is interesting to note though that at this time many Romans had conflicting views of writers and poets. On the one hand it was good to cultivate the mind and reading and writing was an excellent hobby for relaxation, but it also could make "libertines" out of men who became to flippant with all the extra time they had for leisure and pleasure.

In the late Republic, many people viewed reading as a suitable hobby and the mark of an educated Roman. Romans had their own libraries and purchased books from local bookstores in various sections of Rome. Public libraries existed where people could check-out a book for a period of time from the vast volume of works in Latin and Greek. Romans could also learn of the latest literary works or poetry at parties as this was a popular form of entertainment. Because poetry was meant to be sung or chanted aloud, poets would go to parties just to sing their works to grateful audiences.

Thus, it could have happened that on one occasion at a party in Messalla's house the young Sulpicia was encouraged to sing one of her elegies to the guests. Perhaps her elegies were deemed worthy enough to be written down and thence forth published. Though this part of her life remains a mystery, what isn't a mystery is the fact that her works were preserved alongside Tibullus'. For one reason or another, her works were considered worthy of being preserved alongside one of Rome's well praised Neoteric poets. This is undoubtedly a tribute to her abilities as a poet.

It would only seem obvious that her writings would display some sort of resemblance to Tibullus' writings. However her poetry and style resemble to a small extent Catullus, but to a larger extent are distinctly her own. Where Tibullus prefers the secluded quiet life in the countryside, Sulpicia, like Catullus, desires a life in the hustle and bustle of the city. Like Catullus' many of her poems about the "love/hate" relationship with Lesbia, Sulpicia has the same type of relationship with her boyfriend Cerinthus.

One distinct aspect of Sulpicia's works involves a unique subject matter. Sulpicia mentions a birthday celebration in two poems. For a Roman, birthdays were an occasion for joyous celebration from plebian to patrician alike. A birthday celebration had as much religious importance as social importance in ancient Rome. The celebration would start with building an alter of turf and flowers and on it would be placed offerings of wine and food. The occasion would call for a large dinner party to which friends and family would be invited and required to be dressed in all white. Birthday honorees would be given gifts from all the guests that attended the party. For Sulpicia and many Romans, spending a birthday apart from loved ones would be an extremely sad occasion.

From this point in her life the historian is left with more questions than answers. There is no record of her life with her ward except the before mentioned. To speculate about the rest of her life would be fruitless. The only historical data that exists from this point on are her words in her poetry. The times in which Sulpicia lived were tumultuous. The role of women in Rome seemed to relax for a time, but then when Augustus became sole ruler of Rome, he began to institute reforms that brought about order to what was a fragile society. It was hard for anyone to escape the laws and reforms set by Augustus. The laws Augustus enacted to restore the Roman population by rewarding families for having as many children as possible, were definitely not in line with Sulpicia's life style. The freedoms women began to enjoy during the late Republic were being erased by Augustus' new reforms. One only needs to examine the life of Ovid to see the punishment of blatantly ignoring the will of the Roman government. History has no record of her life after the poems, perhaps, like Ovid her voice was stamped out by Augustus.

SECTION II

Catullus and His Influence on Sulpicia

Horace once wrote: Graecia capta ferum victorem cepit. (Captured Greece captured her wild conqueror). For Horace and many other learned Romans of the upper class since Rome established complete control of Greece in 197 B.C.E, the Greek or Hellenistic culture possessed many attributes worthy of emulation and admiration. There was no wealthy Roman citizen of the first century B.C.E. who did not know both Greek and Latin. From the time Rome was first brought into contact with the Greek world she began to drink deeply from the springs of Hellenistic culture.[14]

During the first century B.C.E. a poetic movement began to take form as a direct result of this Greek intoxication that scholars refer to as "Neoteric Poetics." This term originated from the Roman orator Cicero when he was describing, with a contemptuous dismissive manner, a group of young poets who had made their way onto the Roman poetic scene with a newer and trendier style of writing.[15] Cicero was a man who dedicated his life to his *patria*. The Rome he knew and loved was great because of the high standards and *pietas* or code of conduct that each Roman citizen cherished and adhered to with the unwavering notion of duty to the sacred fatherland. Without question for Cicero, Latin poetry and literature needed to adhere to these standards that were the fabric of Roman ideals and society. The Greeks were self indulgent, overly leisured, and impractical. They studied art for the sake of art. These traits were not fit for a Roman.

But for Catullus and the other young Neoteric poets, adhering to the literary forms of what embodied Roman *pietas* and Roman standards of educated patricians was something they vehemently detested. They were, like Horace implied, captivated by all things Greek. Thus, the elements of Neoteric poetry, which Cicero and other "practical" Romans detested, were: a highly refined artistic quality based upon Greek poetic meter and rhythm; poetry purposefully designed to be short in length; and a sincere, personal, and "ego" focused theme often with sarcastic and almost outright yet still subtle mockery of society and or people in society. These elements are easily elucidated through the works of Catullus—the ideal embodiment of Neoteric poetry.

The catalyst for creating a refined quality is of course traced to the Greeks, and most specifically the highly influential and often emulated Greek poet Callimachus. Peter Knox, in his article *Catullus and Callimachus*, goes as far as saying that Callimachus, especially in his poetic work *Aetia*, made a big impression on the minds of the Roman poets of the first century B.C.E; this impression for Catullus was deeply grounded in his continual creation of poems which reflected Greek meter.[16] Catullus approaches his first poem through a meter, hendecasyllabic, known in the ancient world as having a vernacular quality and rhythms of street language.[17] In the first two lines of this poem he also embodies what the Neoteric poets sought to do—turn away from the norms of Latin literature of oratory and epic expression, confining their expression to short, succinct written word, perfected with "a highly polished pumice stone."

> *Cui dono lepidum novum libellum*
> *arida modo pumice expolitum?*

Catullus' artistry lies in the endless pursuit to make Latin poetry reflect complex Greek meter. He used hendecasyllabic meter for almost half of his poems. This highly refined and artistic quality of Catullus' poetic works was for Cicero "a repertoire of glittering verbal tricks."[18] But it wasn't simply the meter that Catullus tried to emulate—it was the passionate pursuit to make his works short, sweet, and perfect.

Perhaps for Catullus, the Latin literature of his day and age seemed out of date and not modern enough for his tastes. With ready access to the Greek poets of the third and second centuries B.C.E., Catullus incorporated the qualities of Hellenistic poets like Mimnernus and Meleager, who favored short poems which were erudite, allusive, and polished.[19] W.R. Johnson in his article *Neoteric Poetics* asserts that "they (Neoteric poets) wrote short poems (of varying lengths, of various sorts), ones whose language could be polished and trimmed with a joyous severity" (181). A good example of this is Catullus' poem 85. Again he uses a complex meter to express in few words how his lover drives him insane:

> *Odi et amo. Quare id faciam, fortasse requiris.*
> *Nescio, sed fieri sentio et excrucior*

In this poem Catullus expresses his conflicting emotions over his lover in a brief yet to the point Elegiac couplet. The meter, an Archaic Greek form utilizing one dactylic hexameter followed by a pentameter, is noted to be among Catullus' favorite. In just two lines the reader is struck with the immediacy of Catullus' feelings. He needs only two lines to express his conflicting feelings as the poem not only gets meaning from the language but also from the flow of the meter as it is read aloud.

Because poetry was meant to be read aloud or sung, it makes the final element that much more theatrical and in essence Greek. The infusion of Catullus' own feelings and emotions makes it easy for the recite and the listener to feel his emotions. There are many sincere, personal and "ego" focused themes found in Catullus' poems. The first evidence of a personal and sincere element lies again in Catullus' first poem where he seeks to mimic the greatest Greek influence. In Callimachus' prologue of *Aetia*, he appeals to his friends and critics and then proceeds to have discourse with the Muses.[20] Emulating Callimachus' style, Catullus creates the same type of discourse in his poem:

> *cui dono lepidum novum libellum*
> *arida modo pumice expolitum?*
> *Corneli, tibi namque tu solebas*

By line three Catullus makes an appeal to his friend, Cornelius, to accept his little book of poetry. Catullus continues to assert that Cornelius is the only one who truly understands his writings. In creating a dedication or appeal of acceptance to a friend in his poetry, Catullus has deterred from the Latin norm and emulated a more personal, sincere convection for his poetry. Where Cicero and other Roman statesmen found it only appropriate to convey such ideas in letters or pamphlets, Catullus did so in his poetry, following the Greek style perfected by Callimachus.[21]

Many times Catullus allows the reader to enter his world, a world where the first person voice is injected and exposed. He becomes the subject and his voice seems to be heartfelt and genuine. He displayed every emotion from bliss to despair, from self-pity to outrage and mockery.[22] Never mind the fact that Catullus, a Roman male citizen, candidly expressed his feelings of love and affection for a woman; most notably his poems addressed to Lesbia, his lover, or in some instances women he desired, this form of expression was not commonplace in Ancient Roman literature. However, these personal poems were a foundation for future poets to convey their own passions and emotions in Latin through what was at first a Greek method. In poem 32 Catullus quickly injects his "ego" with a request to a woman of less reputable character, perhaps a prostitute:

> *Amabo, mea dulcis Ipsitilla,*
> *meae deliciae, mi lepores,*
> *iube ad te veniam meridiatum*

Here Catullus requests that his sweet Ipsitilla remain with him for an afternoon siesta. Though Catullus' request at first seems innocent, this request for an afternoon nap doesn't merely imply rest and relaxation, but rather a long sexual encounter:

> *sed domi maneas paresque nobis*
>
> *novem continuas fututiones*

In this poem not only does Catullus openly expose and mock the Roman tradition that encounters of this kind during mid-day were taboo and unclean, Catullus, the embodiment of Neoteric poetics, audaciously voiced his desires and sarcastically mocked Roman superstitions. This candid expression wasn't a Roman tradition. Catullus was a learned man, the doctus of his time; he was undoubtedly influenced and captivated by the Greek predecessors Mimnernus and Meleager. These Hellenists had given him the platform and model in which to express himself.[23]

Everything about Catullus' poetry reflected his captivation and subjugation to the Greek stylistic forms and aesthetics. He came from a wealthy patrician family where he undoubtedly received a well rounded education in Latin and Greek. He was Roman, filled with passion, who found a model for expressing himself through the once exclusively Hellenistic literary ideals of the liberation of the mind, the body, and the soul—because there was no other model in Latin to emulate. What drove him to create Latin poetry that reflected Greek influences was the practicality that Latin, until his time, was impractical—it had little poetic traditions for expressing the daily emotions a person experienced.

Like Catullus, Sulpicia had access to a good education grounded in the Greek poetics. With the level of her education, she undoubtedly read the same Greek works that Catullus had. It is clear that Catullus' works had an impact on Sulpicia. Her poetic style is not only a reflection of Catullus' style but it also embodied Neoteric poetics as she turned away from the norms of Latin literature of oratory and epic expression instead writing short, succinct poems of love, passion, and vulnerability.

SECTION III

SULPICIAE ELEGIAE

ROMAN ELEGY

Sulpicia's poems are love elegies. They are written in elegiac couplets and they are about love and reflect an independent woman's voice. First begun in Greece and emulated by Rome, the elegiac couplet was originally used for short poems, including epigrams for dedications or on funeral monuments.[24] Ovid, Propertius, Tibullus and Gallus all wrote collections of elegiac couplets. Some consider Gallus to be the most important writer of elegies but none of his works survive. Ovid's Ars Amatoria and Amores are the most liked and well known of the elegiac genre. Sulpicia stands out from her contemporaries not only because she was a woman, but because her elegies are considerably shorter than the Tibullus' or Ovid's elegies. In this way her works best reflect Catullus' influence (Poems 70, 75, 79, 82 and 85 to name a few are short and succinct elegies). In fact, for Catullus, elegiac couplets are his favorite form of poetry, used in poems 65-116.[25]

Because Latin poetry was meant to be read aloud or even sung, it is important to understand that meter is the rhythm of poetry. The meter in her poems is **elegiac couplet**, with the first line a **dactylic hexameter** (six sets or feet of either one long syllable, followed by another long syllable, or one long syllable followed by two short syllables) followed in the second line by a slower **pentameter**. The stress of the last syllable in a line can be left for the reader to accentuate.

Common rules for scansion are:

Elision -- a word ending in a vowel elides with the next word if it begins with a vowel. A final *m* and a beginning *h* are ignored as a phonetic element and elided. [26] There are only six elisions in all of Sulpicia's poems: one in ***Tandem Venit Amor***, one in ***Dies Sine Cerintho***, and four in ***Gratum Est***.

Example: In line two, *atque Arrentino*, the *e* at the end of *atque* would be elided, *atqu(e)*, and be read as one word *atquArrentino*.

Long by Nature -- A vowel is long by nature if it is a member of a diphthong: *ae, au, ei, eu, oe*, and *ui*.

Long by Position -- A vowel by position if it is followed by two consonants: the first *i* in *trīstis*. This rule applies to vowels that are followed by two consonants even if the vowel and consonant are in a different word.

Exceptions to this rule are:
>   *x* is *cs* and counts as two consonants.
>   *z* is *dz* and counts as two consonants.
>   *i* at the beginning of a word, like *iam*, counts as one consonant
>   *j*.(Note *i* should not be elided.)
>   *qu* counts as one consonant.
>   As stated above, *h* is not counted as a consonant.

Syncopation -- the shortening of a perfect or pluperfect active verb for the purpose of meter.

Example: *optarim* for *optaverim* in poem ***Calor Tuae Puellae***.

TANDEM VENIT AMOR

Sulpicia writes of her new found abilities as a poet and her new found love.

Tandem venit amor, qualem texisse pudori
quam nudasse alicui sit mihi fama magis.
Exorata meis illum Cytherea Camenis
adtulit in nostrum deposuitque sinum.
Exsolvit promissa Venus: mea gaudia narret,
dicetur siquis non habuisse sua.
Non ego signatis quicquam mandare tabellis,
ne legat id nemo quam meus ante, velim,
sed peccasse iuvat, vultus conponere famae
taedet: cum digno digna fuisse ferar.

NOTES

pudori, mihi double dative (dative of purpose, dative of reference)

Cytherea is the Greek Aphrodite or Latin Venus

Camenis are the Roman version of the Muses, i.e. poetry. Sulpicia's poetry
has won her the affection of her boyfriend

illum is Cerinthus

depono put down, plant, entrust for safekeeping

siquis if anyone

signatis quicquam mandare tabellis use **non** and translate as "she wishes
she did not have to seal up her writings"

quam ... ante is antequam

meus my own true love

taedet it wearies me...

ferar may I be said/reported to...

QUESTIONS

Parse the following words: *dicetur, tabellis, legat, vultus* and *famae.*

Explain how Sulpicia feels in this poem and her reasons for feeling this way?

Explain how from this poem we can verify that Sulpicia was either a patrician or from a wealthy family?

DIES SINE CERINTHO

In this poem the reader is introduced to two influential people in Sulpicia's life:

> *Messalla and Cerinthus.*
> *Invisus natalis adest, qui rure molesto*
> *et sine Cerintho tristis agendus erit.*
> *Dulcius urbe quid est? an villa sit apta puellae*
> *atque Arrentino frigidus amnis agro?*
> *Iam nimium Messalla mei studiose, quiescas,*
> *heu tempestivae, saeve propinque, viae!*
> *Hic animum sensusque meos abducta relinquo,*
> *arbitrio quamvis non sinis esse meo.*

NOTES

urbe ablative of comparison

amnis river, stream

Messalla this is her guardian

mei objective genitive with studiose

iam quiescas "Now give it a rest."

tempestivae early, seasonable, in season

propinquus near

heu translate as non

arbitrium judgment, control

QUESTIONS

Parse the following words: *urbe, Cerintho, viae, erit, quiescas* and *Messalla.*

Explain how Sulpicia feels in this poem and her reasons for feeling this way?

Explain how from this poem how we can verify that Sulpicia was either a patrician or from a wealthy family?

Bonus: Sulpicia mentions a country home in **Arrentino** located in a gorgeous modern day vacation spot in Italy known as what? (Hint: the area is famous for pottery-- Arezzo.)

TRISTE ITER SUBLATUM

Sulpicia expresses her joy over being able to attend Cerinthus' birthday celebration.

> *Scis iter ex animo sublatum triste puellae?*
> *natali Romae iam licet esse suo.*
> *Omnibus ille dies nobis natalis agatur,*
> *qui nec opinanti nunc tibi forte venit.*

NOTES

Scis refers to Cerinthus

triste modifies **iter**

qui -- antecedent is **dies**

QUESTIONS

Parse the following words: *scis, puellae, venit, iter, Romae* and *animo.*

Why was Sulpicia sad?

Will there be many people at Cerinthus' supposed birthday celebration?

Why do you think birthdays were so important to the Romans?

Calor Tuae Puellae

In this poem, Sulpicia seems to be perplexed with Cerinthus' insensitivity.

Estne tibi, Cerinthe, tuae pia cura puellae,
quod mea nunc vexat corpora fessa calor?
A ego non aliter tristes evincere morbos
optarim, quam te si quoque velle putem.
At mihi quid prosit morbos evincere, si tu
nostra potes lento pectore ferre mala?

NOTES

tuae puellae translate "for ..."

calor fever (of passion or illness)

aliter otherwise

optarim this verb is syncopated and is optaverim, subjunctive

prosit subjunctive

QUESTIONS

Parse the following words: *prosit, vexat, lentus, corpora, calor.*

Does **calor** refer to the physical body only? Explain.

Does Sulpicia doubt Cerinthus' feelings for her? Explain.

Me Paenitet Hesternam Noctem

Sulpicia regrets her decision to leave Cerinthus alone the previous night.

Ne tibi sim, mea lux, aeque iam fervida cura
ac videor paucos ante fuisse dies,
si quicquam tota conmisi stulta iuventa,
cuius me fatear paenituisse magis,
hesterna quam te solum quod nocte reliqui,
ardorem cupiens dissimulare meum.

NOTES

sim optative subjunctive

ante ago, before

ac as

tota iuventa ablative (of time within which)

stulta nominative

conmisi I brought about

cuius objective genitive with paenituisse

dissimulare to conceal

QUESTIONS

Parse the following words: *lux, videor, nocte, cupiens.*

What does Sulpicia call Cerinthus in the first line? Explain.

Does Sulpicia give a clue about her age in this poem? Explain.

What does Sulpicia regret?

APPENDICES

APPENDIX I

When I received the news of your daughter Tullia's death, I was indeed as much grieved and distressed as I was bound to be, and looked upon it as a calamity in which I shared. For, if I had been at home, I should not have failed to be at your side, and should have made my sorrow plain to you face to face. That kind of consolation involves much distress and pain, because the relations and friends, whose part it is to offer it, are themselves overcome by an equal sorrow. They cannot attempt it without many tears, so that they seem to require consolation themselves rather than to be able to afford it to others. Still I have decided to set down briefly for your benefit such thoughts as have occurred to my mind, not because I suppose them to be unknown to you, but because your sorrow may perhaps hinder you from being so keenly alive to them.

Why is it that a private grief should agitate you so deeply? Think how fortune has hitherto dealt with us. Reflect that we have had snatched from us what ought to be no less dear to human beings than their children—country, honor, rank, every political distinction. What additional wound to your feelings could be inflicted by this particular loss? Or where is the I that should not by this time have lost all sensibility and learned to regard everything else as of minor importance? Is it on her account, pray, that you sorrow? How many times have you recurred to the thought—and I have often been struck with the same idea—that in times like these theirs is far from being the worst fate to whom it has been granted to exchange life for a painless death? Now what was there

33

at such an epoch that could greatly tempt her to live? What scope, what hope, what I's solace? That she might spend her life with some young and distinguished husband? How impossible for a man of your rank to select from the present generation of young men a son-in-law, to whose honor you might think yourself safe in trusting your child! Was it that she might bear children to cheer her with the sight of their vigorous youth? Who might by their own character maintain the position handed down to them by their parent, might be expected to stand for the offices in their order, might exercise their freedom in supporting their friends? What single one of these prospects has not been taken away before it was given? But, it will be said, after all it is an evil to lose one's children. Yes, it is: only it is a worse one to endure and submit to the present state of things.

I wish to mention to you a circumstance which gave me no common consolation, on the chance of its also proving capable of diminishing your sorrow. On my voyage from Asia, as I was sailing from Aegina towards Megara, I began to survey the localities that were on every side of me. Behind me was Aegina, in front Megara, on my right Piraeus, on my left Corinth: towns which at one time were most flourishing, but now lay before my eyes in ruin and decay. I began to reflect to myself thus: "Hah! Do we manikins feel rebellious if one of us perishes or is killed—we whose life ought to be still shorter—when the corpses of so many towns lie in helpless ruin? Will you please, Servius, restrain yourself and recollect that you are born a mortal man?" Believe me, I was no little strengthened by that reflection. Now take the trouble, if you agree with me, to put this thought before your eyes. Not long ago all those most illustrious men perished at one blow: the empire of the Roman people suffered that huge loss: all the provinces were shaken to their foundations. If you have become the poorer by the frail spirit of one poor girl, are you agitated thus violently? If she had not died now, she would yet have had to die a few years hence, for she was mortal born. You, too, withdraw soul and thought from such things, and rather remember those which become the part you have played in life: that she lived as long as life had anything to give her; that her life outlasted that of the Republic; that she lived to see you—her own father—

praetor, consul, and augur; that she married young men of the highest rank; that she had enjoyed nearly every possible blessing; that, when the Republic fell, she departed from life. What faults have you or she to find with fortune on this score? In fine, do not forget that you are Cicero, and a man accustomed to instruct and advise others; and do not imitate bad physicians, who in the diseases of others profess to understand the art of healing, but are unable to prescribe for themselves. Rather suggest to yourself and bring home to your own mind the I maxims which you are accustomed to impress upon others. There is no sorrow beyond the power of time at length to diminish and soften: it is a reflection on you that you should wait for this period, and not rather anticipate that result by the aid of your wisdom. But if there is any consciousness still existing in the world below, such was her love for you and her dutiful affection for all her family, that she certainly does not wish you to act as you are acting. Grant this to her—your lost one! Grant it to your friends and comrades who mourn with you in your sorrow! Grant it to your country, that if the need arises she may have the use of your services and advice.

Finally—since we are reduced by fortune to the necessity of taking precautions on this point also—do not allow anyone to think that you are not mourning so much for your daughter as for the state of public affairs and the victory of others. I am ashamed to say any more to you on this subject, lest I should appear to distrust your wisdom. Therefore I will only make one suggestion before bringing my letter to an end. We have seen you on many occasions bear good fortune with a noble dignity which greatly enhanced your fame: now is the time for you to convince us that you are able to bear bad fortune equally well, and that it does not appear to you to be a heavier burden than you ought to think it. I would not have this be the only one of all the virtues that you do not possess.

As far as I am concerned, when I learn that your mind is more composed, I will write you an account of what is going on here, and of the condition of the province.

APPENDIX II

Yes, indeed, my dear Servius, I would have wished, as you say, that you had been by my side at the time of my grievous loss. How much help your presence might have given me, both by consolation and by your taking an almost equal share in my sorrow, I can easily gather from the fact that after reading your letter I experienced a great feeling of relief. For not only was what you wrote calculated to soothe a mourner, but in offering me consolation you manifested no slight sorrow of I yourself. Yet, after all, your son Servius by all the kindnesses of which such a time admitted made it evident, both how much he personally valued me, and how gratifying to you he thought such affection for me would be. His kind offices have of course often been pleasanter to me, yet never more acceptable. For myself again, it is not only your words and (I had almost said) your partnership in my sorrow that consoles me, it is your character also. For I think it a disgrace that I should not bear my loss as you—a man of such wisdom—think it should be borne. But at times I am taken by surprise and scarcely offer any resistance to my grief, because those consolations fail me, which were not wanting in a similar misfortune to those others, whose examples I put before my eyes. For instance, Quintus Maximus, who lost a son who had been consul and was of illustrious character and brilliant achievements, and Lucius Paullus, who lost two within seven days, and your kinsman Gallus and M. Cato, who each lost a son of the highest character and valor-- all lived in circumstances which permitted their own great position, earned by their public services, to assuage their grief. In my case, after losing

36

the honors which you yourself mention, and which I had gained by the greatest possible exertions, there was only that one solace left which has now been torn away. My sad musings were not interrupted by the business of my friends, or by the management of public affairs: there was nothing I cared to do in the forum: I could not bear the sight of the senate-house; I thought—as was the fact—that I had lost all the fruits both of my industry and of fortune. But while I thought that I shared these losses with you and certain others, and while I was conquering my feelings and forcing myself to bear them with patience I had a refuge, one bosom where I could find repose, one in whose conversation and sweetness I could lay aside all anxieties and sorrows. But now, after such a crushing blow as this, the wounds which seemed to have healed break out afresh. For there is no republic now to offer me a refuge and a consolation by its good fortunes when I leave my home in sorrow, as there once was a home to receive me when I returned saddened by the state of public affairs. Hence I absent myself both from home and forum, because home can no longer console the sorrow which public affairs cause me, nor public affairs that which I suffer at home. All the more I look forward to your coming, and long to see you as soon as possible. No reasoning can give me greater solace than a renewal of our intercourse and conversation. However, I hope your arrival is approaching, for that is what I am told. For myself, while I have many reasons for wishing to see you as soon as possible, there is this one especially—that we may discuss beforehand on what principles we should live through this period of entire submission to the will of one man who is at once wise and liberal, far, as I think I perceive, from being hostile to me, and very friendly to you. But though that is so, yet it is a matter for serious thought what plans, I don't say of action, but of passing a quiet life by his leave and kindness, we should adopt. Good-bye.

APPENDIX III

CICERO'S REQUEST FOR SERVIUS SULPICIUS RUFUS' PUBLIC FUNERAL

And as Servius Sulpicius Rufus, the son of Quintus of the Lemonian tribe, has deserved so well of the republic as to be entitled to be complimented with all those distinctions; the senate is of opinion, and thinks it for the advantage of the Republic, that the consule aedile should suspend the edict which usually prevails with respect to funerals in the case of the funeral of Servius Sulpicius Rufus, the son of Quintus of the Lemonian tribe; and that Caius Pansa, the consul, shall assign him a place for a tomb in the Esquiline plain, or in whatever place shall seem good to him, extending thirty feet in every direction, where Servius Sulpicius may be buried; and that that shall be his tomb, and that of his children and posterity, as having been a tomb most deservedly given to them by the public authority."

NOTES

1. Both historians and archeologists are unable to locate her exact birthplace and residence, but through subtleties in her own writings and information available about her father, mother, and extended family, this is the most accurate place of birth and residence throughout her life.
2. See Appendix I for this *Letter of Consolation* Servius Sulpicius Rufus wrote to Cicero.
3. See Appendix II *Cicero's Letter in Response* to Servius' Condolence letter after the death of Tullia, Cicero's daughter.
4. See Appendix II
5. In this book the poems have been given appropriate titles. The traditional title of this poem is *Poem II.*
6. *Women Latin Poets* page 32.
7. Direct quotation from *Life and Leisure in Ancient Rome,* page 117
8. Cicero's *Ninth Philippic.*
9. See *Dies Cerintho.*
10. Edwars Berwick, *Lives of Marcus Valerius Messala Corvinus and Titus Pomponius Atticus*, 66; Direct Quotation.
11. From Gibbon's *Decline and Fall of the Roman Empire*
12. Berwick, 65
13. Ibid, 62.
14. R.M. Ogilvie, *Roman Literature and Society*, 68
15. W.R. Johnson, *Neoteric Poetics,* 176
16. Peter Knox, *Catullus and Callimachus*, 153
17. Daniel Garrison, *The Student's Catullus*, 178
18. Johnson, 178
19. David Mulroy, *The Complete Poetry of Catullus*, xxviii

20. Ibid, 153; Direct Quotation
21. Ogilvie, 71
22. Ibid, 74; Direct Quotation
23. Ibid, 74
24. See Garrison's Student's Catullus, 175-177
25. Ibid, 175-177
26. Ibid, 177

GLOSSARY

a -- by, at

abducta -- leading away

adsum, adesse -- to be present

aeque -- equally (adv.)

ago, agere -- drive, urge, do

agendus – which ought to be done (future participle)

ager, agri -- field, farm, estate

aliquis, aliquod -- one or the other (pron.)

aliter -- otherwise, else

amor, amoris -- m. love, affection

amnis, is -- river

an -- or, whether

animus, i -- mind, spirit, consciousness

ante -- before, previously (adv.)

aptus, a, um -- tied, bound

arbitrium, i -- power, control

ardor, ardoris -- m. fire, flame, heat

Arrentinus, i -- m. area in Etruria known for its pottery

at -- but

atque -- and

calor, caloris -- fever, zeal

Cerinthus, Cerinthi -- boyfriend of Sulpicia

conpono, conponere -- to arrange, compose, write

corpora, corporis -- body

cum -- with, when

cupio, cupere -- to desire, be eager for

cura, ae -- care, concern, worry

dies, diei-- day

dico, dicere -- to say, talk

digno, dignare – to think worthy

dulcius -- charming (adj.)

ego -- I

estne -- is he/she not?

et -- and

evinco, evincere -- to conquer

ex -- out of

exsolvo, exsolvere – to free, pay off

fama, ae -- f. rumor

fero, ferre -- to carry

fervidus, a, um -- glowing, boiling hot

fessa, ae -- f. tired

forte -- by chance (adv.)

frigidus, a, um -- cold

gaudium, i -- n. joy, delight

habeo, habere -- to have, hold

hesternus, a, um -- of yesterday

hic, haec, hoc -- this (pron.), here (adv.)

iam -- now

ille, illa, illud -- that (adj.), he (pron.)

in -- (prep. w/abl. in, on, at; w/acc. into, about, in the midst of, for)

invisus, a, um – hated, unseen

iter, ineris -- n. journey

iuventas, iuventatis -- f. youth

iuvo, iuvare -- to help, aid, serve

lentus -- slow, easy, indifferent

lego, legare – to bequeath; entrust

lego, legere – to collect; read

licet -- it is permitted

lux, lucis – f. light

magis -- more nearly; rather, instead (adv.)

mala, ae -- f. cheek bone

molestus, a, um -- annoying

me -- me (acc.)

Messalla -- ward and uncle of Sulpicia

meus, mea, meum -- my (adj.), mine (pron.)

mihi -- to me (dat.)

morbus, i -- m. sickness

narrow, narrare -- to tell

natalis -- birthday

ne -- not (adv.)

nec -- neither

nemo, neminis -- m/f. nobody

nimium -- too much, very much

nobis -- to or by us (dat. or abl. plural)

non -- not

noster, stra, strum -- our

nox, noctis -- f. night

nudo, nudare -- lay bare, expose (elision that appears is nudasse for nudavisse)

nunc -- now

omnis, is -- all, everyone

opinanti – conjectures, opinions

opto, optare -- to choose, select

paeniteo, paenitere – to repent, regret, displease

paucus, a, um -- few, little

peco, pecare – to err, do wrong (elision that appears is pecasse for pecavisse)

pectus, oris -- breast, chest

pia, us, um – conscienscious, dutiful

possum, posse -- to be able

promitto, promittere -- promise

propinquus -- near

prosum, prodesse – to be useful, benefit (+ dat.)

pudor, pudoris -- m. decency, shame

puella, ae -- girl

puteo, putere -- to stink

qualis, quale – what kind of (adj

quam -- how, how much

quamvis -- however, ever so

qui -- how or why (adv.), who (pron.)

quicquam -- anyone, any, anything (pron.)

quid -- how?

quiesco, quiescere -- to rest

quod -- because, who (pron.)

quoque -- too

 relinquo, relinquere -- to leave behind

Roma, ae -- Rome

rus, ruris -- the country, countryside

saeve -- fiercely

scio, scire -- to know

sed -- but

sensus, us -- sensation, capacity for feeling

si -- if

sine -- without

sino, sinere -- to allow, permit

sinum, i -- n. a large drinking glass much like a bowl

solus, a, um -- alone, lonely

studiose -- eager or zealous (adv.)

stultus, a, um -- foolish, stupid

sublatum -- (participle of tollo, tollere) to lift or take up

sum, esse -- to be

suo -- to sew or stitch

suus, sua, suum -- one's own (adj.)

tandem -- at last, finally (adv.)

te -- you (acc.)

tego, tegere -- to cover

tempestiva, ae – seasonal, timely, fit

tibi -- you (dat.)

totus, a, um -- whole, all entire

tristis -- sad, sorrowful

tu -- you (nom.)

tua -- your (gen.)

urbs, urbis -- city

velo, velare -- veil, cover

venio, venire -- to come

vexo, vexare -- to vex

via, ae -- road, way

video, videre -- to see; seem

villa, ae -- country home

volo, velle -- to wish

vultus, us -- m. severe facial expression

BIBLIOGRAPHY

Primary Sources

Cicero. *Ad Familiares.*

Cicero. *Fourteen Philippic Orations.*

Plutarch. *Life of Pompey.*

Suetonius. *Life of the Twelve Caesars.*

Tibullus. *Elegies.*

Secondary Sources

Balsdon, J.P.V.D.. *Life and Leisure in Ancient Rome.* (Phoenix Press, London: 1969).

Berwick, Edwars. *Lives of Marcus Velerius Messala Corvinus and Titus Pomponius Atticus.* (James Ballantune and Company, London: 1813).

Cowell, F.R. *Life in Ancient Rome.* (Perigee Books, New York: 1961).

Crawford, Michael. *The Roman Republic.* (Harvard University Press, Cambridge, Massachusetts: 1993).

Cruttwell, Charles. *A History of Roman Literature: From the Earliest Period to Marcus Aurelius.* (Scribner's Sons, New York: 1882).

Garrison, Daniel. *The Student's Catullus.* (U. of Oklahoma Press, Norman: 2004).

Grant, Michael. *Greek and Latin Authors.* (H.W. Wilson and Company, New York: 1980).

Johnson, W.R. "Neoteric Poetics," *Companion to Catullus.* (Blackwell Pub., Malden, MA: 2007).

Knox, Peter. "Catullus and Callimachus," *Companion to Catullus.* (Blackwell Pub., Malden, MA: 2007).

Lee, A.G. *Ovid: Metamorphoses.* (Cambridge University Press: 1953).

Michie, James. The Odes of Horace. (Bobbs-Merrill Company, New York: 1963).

Mulroy, David. *The Complete Works of Catullus.* (U. of Wisconsin, Madison: 2004).

Ogilvie, R.M. *Roman Literature and Society.* (Penguin Books, New York: 1980).

Rawson, Beryl. *Marriage, Divorce, and Children in Ancient Rome.* (Clarendon Press, Oxford: 1996).

Sellar, W.Y. *The Roman Poets of the Republic.* (Clarendon Press, Oxford: 1899).

Printed in the United States
By Bookmasters